Original title:

Citrus Sunrise

Copyright © 2025 Creative Arts Management OÜ
All rights reserved.

Author: Maxwell Donovan
ISBN HARDBACK: 978-1-80586-246-8
ISBN PAPERBACK: 978-1-80586-718-0

Sun Brimming with Citrus Delight

A lemon burst, the morning cheer,
Orange giggles, oh so near.
The zesty rays dance on my face,
In this fruity, sunny place.

Bright tangerines twirl with glee,
Sipping juice from a giddy tree.
Pineapples wearing shades of gold,
Their laughter, oh, it never gets old.

Grapefruit jokes, they make me chuckle,
As limes roll by, they start to puckle.
With every sip, a twist of fate,
A citrus twist, oh, isn't it great?

So raise your glass, don't be shy,
Toast to fruit that catches the eye.
In this merry morning spree,
Every bite's a fruit jubilee!

The Flavor of Dawn Unfurled

In the morning, a burst of cheer,
Lemons dance, they grin ear to ear.
Tangerines giggle as sunlight beams,
Wake up, wake up, it's breakfast dreams!

Oranges roll like playful clowns,
Flipping and flopping, no frowns allowed.
Joyful chaos as flavors collide,
Sipping the smile that mornings provide.

Nature's Golden Zest

The sun yawns wide, a bright little spark,
Lime shows off with a loud, zesty bark.
Grapefruits chuckle, it's quite a scene,
Dancing in sunbeams, like a juice machine.

Bouncing berries join the sun's parade,
Laughing at shadows that quickly fade.
Every color, a pop with delight,
Nature's joke on the fading night.

Dawn's Sweet-tart Embrace

A splash of yellow, a twist of green,
Morning mischief, a lively sheen.
Pineapple's wiggle steals the show,
As cherries giggle, they put on a glow.

Bananas laugh, with peels that fly,
Citrus pranks make the day spry.
Every bite, a silly surprise,
A zest for laughter beneath the skies.

Orchard of Daybreak

Apples blush as the sun sets sail,
Citron struts, telling a tale.
Peeling laughter fills the air,
As laughter bubbles, without a care.

With every squeeze, a giggle escapes,
Fruits in a frenzy, no room for scrapes.
In this orchard, no worries remain,
Just silly splashes of juice and gain.

Warm Hues of Daybreak

The sun pops up like toast, so bright,
With buttered beams that light up the night.
A morning dance of colors so wacky,
The sky's a big fruit bowl, all bright and snappy.

Birds are chirping, a fruity cheer,
While squirrels plot their breakfast near.
Oh, what a morning, so funny and grand,
With zesty laughter across the land.

Peel Back the Morning

Peel back the layers of dreams and fun,
A zesty start under the rising sun.
Juicy giggles drip from the trees,
As the world awakens with a bright squeeze.

Waking up feels like a fruit parade,
With sleepy critters who just charade.
Bananas slip by, singing a tune,
As the daylight struts in, all glimmer and bloom.

Fruitful Beginnings

Morning's here, with a fruity blast,
The day rolls out; it's moving fast.
Jellybeans sky, in shades of surprise,
With jellyfish clouds that wiggle and rise.

Silly squirrels in a jubilant chase,
Dodging the beams in a leafy race.
The sun wears shades, so classic and cool,
As the world signs in, ready for school.

Radiant Oranges in the Sky

Look up at the sky, a citrus delight,
As oranges bounce, refusing to sit tight.
They roll and they giggle, like kids on the run,
Creating a spectacle, oh what fun!

The clouds are fluff, a sweet candy floss,
While the sun flashes smiles, no pain, no loss.
Grab your morning drink, it's a fruity race,
With laughter and joy in the bright embrace.

Toasting the Golden Hour

A glass of juice, so bright and bold,
As orange as a joke retold.
We cheer to dawn with zestful glee,
While sticky fingers dance with tea.

The sun peeks in with a citrus grin,
Knocking at dreams where fun begins.
We wear our hats, a funny sight,
As morning laughs in golden light.

Soft Citrus Caress of Daybreak

A sweet aroma fills the air,
Of tangy dreams and zest to share.
My toast just slipped; it took a dive,
But I still munch—oh, I'm alive!

With lemon drops that skip and twirl,
My sleepy heart begins to whirl.
Orange peels that laugh and play,
Make breakfast bright in a funny way.

Hues of Hope and Citrus

The dawn paints skies in lemon bright,
While giggles bounce with pure delight.
A grapefruit hat, I wear with pride,
As morning sings, I cannot hide.

My breakfast fruit, they laugh and tease,
A banana peel slips with ease.
With every sip, the day grows bold,
A funny tale of joy unfolds.

Orchard Dreams at Dawn

In orchards grand, where laughter flows,
A silly dance is how it goes.
With tangerines tossed just for fun,
We laugh and dodge beneath the sun.

As robins chirp their citrus song,
I stumble once and then I'm strong.
With sticky hands and playful spins,
The day begins as laughter wins.

Nature's Zesty Awakening

Orange globes hang high, oh what a sight,
They dance with joy in the morning light.
Lemon trees giggle, swaying with ease,
While grapefruits blush, whispering to bees.

Birds chirp in tones of sweet, tangy cheer,
As citrus scents tickle your nose, oh dear!
A puppy's bark joins in on this spree,
For nature's fun fair is wild and free.

A Slice of Morning Light

The sun peeks over, with a grin so bright,
It's slicing through clouds like a tasty bite.
A tangerine twist in the sky up high,
With giggles of light as the day passes by.

Pineapple clouds in a fluffy parade,
While the shadows break out in a sunshine charade.
Kites shaped like limes toss the morning air,
As laughter bounces, with fun everywhere.

Vibrant Peels of Dawn

In the morning's embrace, colors collide,
With laughter and zest, we bounce and slide.
A grapefruit wiggles as it rolls off the shelf,
While lime slices giggle, just being themselves.

The dew drops chuckle on orange tree leaves,
As squirrels in hats perform little thieves.
Nature's a circus where joy is the theme,
Under the spotlight of a citrusy dream.

Leafs of Daybreak Dreams

Under a canopy of leafy delight,
The morning awakes, bringing forth pure light.
A lemon tree yawns, stretching so wide,
While herbivores frolic with zest in their stride.

The world is a plate, each flavor a treat,
With bursts of delight in the day's heartbeat.
So raise your glass high to the morning so grand,
For joy is a fruit that's ripe in our hand.

Spectrum of Citrus Light

In the morning glow, fruits are in a race,
Lemon and lime, they're putting on a face.
A grapefruit giggles, a tangerine grins,
While oranges roll, collecting their wins.

Juicy jests fly as the peels take to dance,
A banana slips in for a silly romance.
The oranges toast with a fizzy delight,
While lime slices wink in the golden sunlight.

Shimmering Citrus Awakening

The zesty crew wakes with a giddy cheer,
Limes in bow ties, squeezing out their fear.
Lemons laugh loud, cracking citrusy jokes,
While grapefruits giggle at funky folks.

Dancing on tables with bubblegum flair,
Pineapples twirl, flying through the air.
With each juicy pun, the day starts so bright,
In a world of fruit, everything feels right.

Morning's Zingy Light

As oranges rise in a bright citrus hue,
The zest is alive, and so is the crew.
Joking around while the daylight is fresh,
With lime left to ponder, 'Am I just a mesh?'

A coconuts chime in with nonsensical glee,
Saying, 'Life's worth living, so just let it be!'
Bananas in pajamas are ready to prance,
While grapefruits roll by, leading the dance.

Golden Leaves in the Morning

Under gold leaves, the laughter unfolds,
Each fruit tells a tale, goofy and bold.
Mandarins tease with their ticklish peels,
And lemons share secrets that make everyone squeal.

The sunlight's a comedian on high,
Casting shadows that wobble as time flutters by.
The orchard's alive with its quirky pretense,
As all the fruits giggle in zesty suspense.

Fruity Morning Meditations

A tangerine on my pillow, oh what a sight,
Dreaming of oranges, in morning's soft light.
Peeling back laughter, like layers of skin,
Juicy confessions, let morning begin.

Bananas in pajamas, dancing with glee,
Pineapples chuckling, as fresh as can be.
A grapefruit giggles, as I take a bite,
Fruit salad whispers, 'Let's party tonight!'

Ripening Dreams at Dawn

In a grove where the lemons plot mischief,
Their zesty sarcasm, quite the grift!
Limes do the limbo, with all of their zest,
Citrus convos, oh they're simply the best.

Mimosas in my dreams, mix laughter and cheer,
Orange juice puns, bring breakfast right here.
Squeeze every moment, let joy overflow,
Fruitful adventures, in morning's warm glow.

Dawn Whispers of Lemon

A lemon tree snores, as the sun starts to rise,
Splashing bright laughter in morning skies.
Holding a debate with a curious lime,
"Why are we sour? Let's sweeten with time!"

The morning's enchantment keeps spirits so high,
As lemons contemplate how to flirt with the sky.
"Bring spritz and some sparkle, let's cause a ruckus,
With zesty remarks that come straight from the buskus!"

A Citrus Canvas for the Sky

Painting the heavens with shades of delight,
A blender of colors in playful flight.
Kiwi's amusing tales of a fruit that he met,
With a pear, they danced to a funky duet.

Through rays that tickle, and clouds that tease,
The sun paints a portrait, it's sure to please.
A splash of good humor, a dash of the bright,
Fruitful horizons, making mornings just right.

Citrus-Scented Revelations

Lemons dance a jig on the floor,
Oranges giggle, craving more.
Grapefruits wear hats, quite absurd,
As tangerines whisper, 'Spread the word!'

A lime pranks its friend with a twist,
'I'm zestier!' it says, and the rest can't resist.
In this fruity brawl, laughter shines bright,
While pomelos cheer from the side with delight.

Glittering Fruit in the Sky

In the early glow, a pear takes flight,
With a banana cape—what a silly sight!
Mangoes drape clouds like a fruit bazaar,
While the kiwis shout, 'Look, I'm a star!'

Juicy puns float in the morning air,
As apples gossip without a care.
Pineapples giggle, wearing sunglasses,
In this sky of fruits, nobody harasses.

Mornings Tasting of Sunshine

Awake to the laugh of a zesty delight,
With breakfast bananas, what a cheerful sight!
A smoothie sings tunes of sweet orange cheers,
While strawberries giggle, wiping their tears.

With pancakes adorned like fruity towers,
Toast raises its hand—what a toast of ours!
Every bite tickles, like happiness bowls,
In this sunny feast, we gather our souls.

Vibrance of Fresh Citrus

A tangle of fruit in a colorful mess,
Lemons eye limes, both ready to bless.
While zesty oranges play a funny game,
Their laughter peels away any blame.

With a splash of juice, the day takes a turn,
As grapefruits wink, watch them twist and churn.
In this vibrant dance, each fruit has a say,
Bringing smiles to mornings, come join the fray!

Golden Vistas of Citrus

A lemon tree dressed in gold,
Grows fruits that tickle and scold.
They giggle as they dangle down,
And wearing peels, they jest, not frown.

A grapefruit with a twisty grin,
Challenges the orange to a spin.
They dance in the sun, quite a sight,
Spreading juice with playful delight.

The lime joins in, a zestful sprite,
Kicking and laughing, oh what a sight!
With every slice, a joke unfolds,
In the orchard where laughter molds.

There's a punchline hidden in every bite,
As nature serves up this comic light.
In these golden vistas, so alive,
The silliness of fruit helps us thrive.

Fruitful Light Unveiled

A tangerine in slippers bright,
Sneaks out to play in the warm daylight.
He trips on peels, but can't stop grinning,
We laugh as he keeps on spinning.

Limes are playing hide and seek,
Behind the leaves, they squeak, they peek.
With zestful giggles, they chase around,
Each citrus joke is joyfully found.

An orange thinks he's quite the star,
With sunglasses on, he travels far.
But as he rolls down the grassy slope,
He finds himself in a tangy hope.

Beneath the sun, the fruits confide,
Sharing puns they can't abide.
In this fruitful light, so surreal,
The laughter cultivates what we feel.

In the Presence of Citrus

Awash in a sea of yellow and green,
Fruits frolic, creating a scene.
The oranges wear hats, so spry,
While lemons wink from the apple pie.

A playful lime cracks a joke,
While grapefruits giggle, and friends provoke.
In this orchard of folly and cheer,
Fruits chatter wildly, loud and clear.

The bananas slip with a silly squeak,
Squirting juice, but never weak.
In the presence of citrus glee,
The fruit bowl's joy is the place to be.

With every segment having fun,
This harvest is second to none.
So let's toast with a twist or two,
In this fruity world where dreams come true.

Citrus Blossoms Beneath the Sun

Beneath the sun where laughter grows,
Citrus blossoms share their woes.
A lime in love with a sweet tangerine,
Whispers jokes that are too obscene.

Lemons wear their pithy crowns,
As grapefruits bounce and giggle in gowns.
They give a toast to life's bright hue,
In a citrus world, where nonsense brews.

With zestiness that knows no bounds,
The trees resound with playful sounds.
In this orchard of mirth and cheer,
Fruitful friendships blossom near.

So gather 'round the sunny glade,
Where every critter joins the parade.
Under blossoms, hilarity spills,
In the laughter of fruits, our joy fulfills.

Radiant Morning Orbs

A yellow globe hangs high, with cheer,
Fruit dreams dance and shift, oh dear!
Orange hats on sleepy heads,
Giggles rise from cozy beds.

Juice drips down like sunshine bright,
Pancakes soak in morning light.
Birds in aprons sing a tune,
Mixing laughter with the moon.

Bubbly breezes tickle trees,
Sipping nectar with such ease.
Lemon drops fall, a sugar rain,
Tickling noses, causing pain!

With oranges tucked in every nook,
Lemonade waits, like a storybook.
Marshmallow clouds drift in the sky,
Mornings like these? Oh my, oh my!

Morning's Citrus Serenade

Whistling winds from fruity lands,
Where every laugh is in demand.
Gather 'round the zesty feast,
The jester's here, the king is pleased!

Banana peels slip on the floor,
Who knew fun could taste like more?
Grapefruit giggles in the bowl,
Tickling ribs and warming souls.

Sunshine pops like candy treats,
Juicy jokes and rhythmic beats.
Let's zest up this sleepy town,
With smiles that never let us down!

Lemons roll like bowling balls,
While laughter echoes off the walls.
Squeezed from joy and cut with sass,
These mornings surely are a blast!

Sunbeam Slices

Chopping sunbeams on the deck,
Careful not to cause a wreck!
Mandarins in playful rows,
Nibbled on as humor grows.

Slithering peels dance and twirl,
While giggling brightens every swirl.
Squishy smiles and fruity cheer,
The morning's kaleidoscope is here!

Balloons tied to the orange tree,
Floating high and feeling free.
Laughs mix with the morning air,
As light plays tag without a care.

Citrus halos round the sun,
A funny game has just begun.
Slice of laughter, zest of glee,
Sunlit mornings, wild and free!

Tangerine Skies Taking Flight

Up above, those tangerine clouds,
Comedic shapes that laugh so loud.
Every sip of bright juice shared,
Sunrise promises, fully prepared.

Funky fruit boots stomp around,
In a jig on this merry ground.
Orange streaks racing through the blue,
A laugh-a-thon for me and you!

Chasing shadows on the grass,
While silly squirrels just zip and pass.
Flavor rockets zoom and glide,
On this yellow joyride wide.

So here we sit with zestful souls,
Jesting up our breakfast goals.
Tangerine skies, our hearts take flight,
Laughter wrapped in morning light!

A Palette of Orange and Yellow

The sun spilled juice on my breakfast plate,
Mimosa mayhem, oh what a fate!
Squeeze the lemon, dance with glee,
These wobbly legs, not mine, but my tea.

A tangerine juggled by my cat,
He hit it once, then glanced at that!
Swiped it off the table with glee,
Now it's rolling, oh silly spree!

Peeling oranges, a slippery mess,
My hands are sticky, I must confess.
But laughter rises, no need to pout,
Stick to the fruit and throw the doubt!

Juicy giggles fill the air,
Fruit salad fun, without a care!
So here's to mornings, bright and bold,
With every slice, a story told!

Sunlit Citrus Cascades

Morning light bounces off the floor,
I tripped on citrus, oh what a chore!
Mandarins rolling under my feet,
Who knew breakfast could be so sweet?

Lemonade laughter, it's splashed on my shoe,
How do I drink that? It's too fun to chew!
A giant grapefruit bounces away,
Chasing it down is my workout play!

Tart and sweet, a zesty game,
Oranges smiling, who's to blame?
I slipped again on a slice that fell,
Laughing so hard, I could barely tell!

Juggling fruits became the plan,
A comedy act, and I'm the man!
With citrus splashes and giggles galore,
Sunlit cascades, who could ask for more?

Lively Morning Zing

Awake to the scent of zest so bright,
Orange alarm clocks, pure delight!
My toast is dancing, what a surprise,
Jam spills sticky, right on my thighs.

Tumbling bananas, oh what a sight,
Funky fruit dance-off, morning so bright!
Lemon drops laughing, if they could,
Making pockets of sunshine, how good!

Grapefruit giggles, they pop and they snap,
One rolled away, what a great nap!
A juicer's wild, it's a party machine,
Pouring out laughter, and plenty of green.

So here's to breakfast, oh what a fling,
With playful fruits, let our laughter ring!
A lively start, where joy takes flight,
Mornings so bright, everything feels right!

Citrus Horizons Meeting Day

The horizon glows with a playful cheer,
Zesty sunrises, laughter is near.
Fruits in the sky, what a funny sight,
They swirl around, oh what pure delight!

A punch of flavor, a giggle, a squeeze,
This orange sky makes my worries freeze.
Limes do a jig, and lemons all cheer,
A citrus rave, come join us, my dear!

Morning cocktails in toasty hues,
With chuckles and fruit, it's all good news!
Tart and zany, what a fun play,
Juicing up the world, hip-hip-hooray!

So let's embrace this vibrant display,
Where every bite keeps the blues at bay.
With laughter and brightness, the world is my stage,
On this citrus horizon, let's flip the page!

A Burst of Citrus Joy

A twist of lemon in my drink,
Makes every sip a bit of kink.
Limes wear hats, so bright and green,
Twirling round like a breakfast scene.

Oranges giggle on the tree,
Rolling down, they call for me.
A citrus dance on morning air,
Juicy fun is everywhere!

Scratching zest beneath my nose,
Sour faces, laughter flows.
Lemonade and giggles shared,
Silly peels, all unprepared.

Bright zest spreads from shore to shore,
Each slice a knock-knock at the door.
So let's toast with a laugh, cheers!
To citrus joy and silly years!

Twilights of Zest

In twilight's glow, a tangerine,
Begins a waltz—what a fine scene!
Purple skies dance with zesty dreams,
Where laughter bubbles like fizzy creams.

Lemon drops fall from the moon,
Tripping up to a silly tune.
Grapefruit grins with a wink so sly,
Cracking jokes as stars go by.

As night descends, so sweet and bright,
Those peels start giggling in delight.
A zestful chase, the night is young,
In the funky fruit song we've sung.

At dawn the laughter breaks the gloom,
Zesty squabbles fill the room.
With every sip and every bite,
The twilight twirls, oh what a sight!

Daylight Citrus Tango

In morning's light, a silly flare,
Oranges burst with zest to share.
A tango danced with citrus glee,
Swaying under the sunny tree.

Lemons split and do the twist,
While grapefruits hike and jiggle, missed.
A yellow sunbeams' limbo line,
When breakfast's bright, the day's divine.

Bananas waltz with cheeky flair,
Chasing limes round without a care.
In this fruit fiesta, laughter sings,
As every juicy moment springs.

A citrus spin that steals the show,
Where sunny smiles just overflow.
Let's dance until the sun goes down,
In our grove of joy, wear the crown!

Refreshing Rays at Break of Day

With dawn's first rays, the fruits arise,
A citrus crew beneath the skies.
Grapes in sunglasses brave the sun,
Sipping juice till day is done.

Lemons ride the morning breeze,
Waving bright like cheerleaders' ease.
Tart and sweet, they kick and shout,
Making sure there's no doubt.

Limes in leaps, and oranges roll,
Chasing laughter, racing soul.
Peeling back the waking dreams,
In this breakfast dance, joy beams.

So here's to zest, so vibrant and loud,
Making moments in the crowd.
With shared giggles in every ray,
A refreshing start to a playful day!

Flavors of the Rising Sun

In the morning, bright and zesty,
A fruit parade feels so festive.
Tangerines dance, lemons play,
All my worries fade away.

With oranges juggling on the breeze,
I laugh at squirrels climbing trees.
Pineapples twirl in a fruit ballet,
Nature's circus starts the day.

Limes make faces, cute and round,
While grapefruits bounce upon the ground.
They whisper jokes without a sound,
As morning laughter spins around.

So grab a slice, enjoy the ride,
With every bite, humor's our guide.
In fruity fun, let spirits soar,
A day so sweet, we'll crave for more.

Nectarine Whisper at Dawn

The sun peeks up with a wink and grin,
As nectarines promise a fruity win.
They giggle softly, oh so sweet,
While honey drops dance to the beat.

Bananas slide, they take a chance,
Beneath a sky of orange pants.
Peaches toss jokes in the air,
Laughter lingers everywhere.

Apricots wink from the tree,
"Mornings taste better with glee!"
Birds chirp back, a playful tune,
Enchanted by this fruity boon.

So let's sip juice, chilled and bright,
While sunrays join in our delight.
With laughter ripening like a pear,
Morning magic is everywhere.

Sunlit Citrus Reverie

Awake in a world of sunny cheer,
Sour surprises are certainly near.
Lemons giggle as they roll about,
While clementines cheer with a shout.

Grapefruit jests, a peel gone wild,
Sunshine frolics, the day beguiled.
Life's a comedy, juicy and bold,
With laughter wrapped in tangerine gold.

The zest of life, a citrus show,
Oranges argue about the glow.
In this pastel playground of bright,
Every moment's a juicy delight.

Beneath the sun's warm embrace,
All the fruits join in a race.
So let's celebrate, come what may,
In this funny fruit soirée.

Luminous Lemons in the Sky

Lemons float like UFOs so grand,
Whisking humor across the land.
Lime aliens land with a quirky shout,
"We come in peace, let's laugh it out!"

Sunlight sparkles on orange dreams,
A citrus world bursting at the seams.
The tarts and sweets, a fruity blend,
In this comedy, we'll never end.

Juicy jokes roll like a ball,
Bouncing higher, having a ball.
With a splash of zest in the air,
They tickle our funny bones with flair.

So gather all the fruits, you see,
Let laughter grow like a lemon tree.
In the sky where giggles fly,
Life's a punchline, oh my, oh my!

Amber Juices of Morning Light

The orange orb peeks from the sky,
A round orange slice, oh me, oh my!
Birds chirp sweet tunes, a zesty cheer,
While squirrels hoard snacks, they're ready to smear.

In the kitchen, a dance with a peel,
A splash of juice, oh what a meal!
Pancakes stacked high, syrup's a dream,
Like citrus confetti, a breakfast theme.

Sunbeams and Tangy Tastes

A squirt of lemon, what a surprise,
Tickling my tongue, oh my, how it flies!
With every sip, I giggle and grin,
Morning shenanigans, let the fun begin!

Limes rolling around, having a ball,
Telling their tales, they bounce off the wall.
Grapefruits gossip, all juicy and round,
Sipping on sunshine, oh, what a sound!

Sunrise in a Juicy Palette

Marmalade skies greet me with zest,
I wear a smile, I'm feeling the best!
Tangerine dreams dance on the floor,
All this fruit humor, who could want more?

Pineapples chuckle, all spiky and bright,
Coconuts laugh, it's a whimsical sight.
A smoothie spills out, it's sliding away,
As I trip on a banana, it's a fruity ballet!

Soft Citrus Hues Awakening

Morning arrives with a splash and a pop,
The zest of the day makes my heart hop!
With grapefruity giggles, I watch in delight,
As oranges roll over, all round and bright.

A splash of lime tickles my nose,
While fruity jokes in the sunlight do pose.
With each little sip, the laughter ignites,
Bringing joy bright and sweet, oh what a sight!

Morning's Citrus Symphony

A lemon waved its arm so bright,
The orange laughed, what a sight!
The grapefruit danced, oh what a sound,
While limes rolled around, joyfully found.

Juicy jokes in the morning air,
Pineapple's hair, a messy affair!
Peeling puns with every slice,
Tangy giggles, oh so nice!

An orchard filled with laughter and cheer,
Even the banana let out a cheer!
Sipping juice mixed with glee,
A fruity party, wild and free!

So join the fun, don't be shy,
The zest of life will make you fly!
In this symphony of bright delight,
You'll find joy, from morning 'til night.

Zesty Horizons

Underneath the sunny glow,
Citrus fruits began to row.
Lemons were captains, bold and loud,
While mandarins formed a cheerful crowd.

Oranges rolled with zestful glee,
Grapefruits joined in a merry spree!
Each slice sang, a fruity tune,
Dancing along to a sweet cartoon.

One lime cracked jokes, oh what a thrill,
While lemons juggled, just for the thrill!
Citrus sauce splattered all around,
In this colorful chaos, joy was found!

As morning light began to break,
Fruits laughed harder, for goodness' sake!
With laughter bright, they chased the day,
In zesty horizons where fun holds sway.

Melodies of Morning Fruit

Peeling oranges sent tunes that swayed,
Amidst the fruit, the laughter played.
Bananas slipped with giggles bright,
While apples twirled in morning light.

Grapefruit crooned a silly song,
Pineapple joined, it felt so wrong!
Lemons zapped with tart retorts,
As cherries jived in goofy shorts.

Zesty jams were spread with glee,
Donuts danced, oh can't you see?
Syrups drizzled, joy on the plate,
Fruits made breakfast feel like fate!

With melodies that bounced and spun,
Who knew mornings could be so fun?
In this fruity symphony of zest,
Every bite's a laugh, truly the best!

Citrus Blooms and Waking Dreams

In a garden where the fruits would play,
Citrus blooms brightened the day.
A tangerine twirled in the breeze,
While oranges giggled, oh what a tease!

Lemons told jokes, sour yet sweet,
Bouncing about with joyful feet.
Grapefruits sang, their skins aglow,
As limey haters put on a show!

Morning dreams floated high and wide,
In a fruit-filled fiesta, joy couldn't hide.
Bananas slipped, but not in despair,
For laughter grows in fruity air!

So gather 'round, let the fun begin,
With waking dreams where all can win.
In this garden of yesterdays beams,
Life is a dance of citrus dreams!

The Glow of Orchard Dreams

A bumblebee with tiny shoes,
Danced among the lemon hues.
He tripped and fell, oh what a scene,
A sticky mess, sweet and keen.

Sunshine splashed like a prankster bright,
Chasing the shadows with all its might.
An orange rolled like a laughing child,
In the orchard, nature's wild.

Pickles flew from the branches high,
As fruits plotted under the sky.
A grapefruit yelled, "I'm the king!"
While limes just laughed at everything.

The trees giggled with green delight,
As squirrels held a fruit fight at night.
With every splash of morning cheer,
The orchard whispers, "Fun is here!"

Citrus-Kissed Morning Glow

A marmalade tiger stretched with glee,
Riding on clouds of tangerine spree.
He tickled the sun, what a cheeky sprite,
Lighting the world with citrus light.

Lemons wore hats, all jaunty and fun,
While oranges giggled, "We're number one!"
Grapefruits tossed a sunrise toast,
To those who love morning the most.

On the breeze, a zesty tune,
Dancing with the lilting noon.
A peach in sunglasses, oh so cool,
Said, "Join the fun, it's our golden rule!"

So let your worries slip away,
Join the laughter, come what may.
In this orchard of light and cheer,
Each dawn's embrace brings fun near.

Dawn's Tangy Embrace

The sun peeked in with a playful wink,
Orange juice spilled, wild as you think.
Lemons rolled with giggles galore,
Squirrels joined in, craving more.

A morning breeze, ticklish and bold,
Sang to the fruits of yellow and gold.
With every ray, a fruit-shaped jest,
In this orchard, life's the best.

The lime decided a joke it would tell,
"Mimosa time? More like a citric spell!"
Bananas laughed till they slipped right down,
In this wacky circus, no room for a frown.

So gather your smiles, embrace the day,
In this tangy world, come out and play.
A zestful life flows in each burst,
As laughter and fruit quench every thirst.

Orchard Whispers at Daybreak

In the orchard where laughter rose,
A lemon tree wore a comical pose.
It juggled fruits like a circus act,
While cherries whispered with a playful pact.

Bright rays of sunshine bounced about,
Tickling tangerines, leaving no doubt.
Peaches giggled at the morning's gleam,
"Oh what a joy! What a fruity dream!"

The nectarines, all dressed in flair,
Threw a party in the open air.
They danced around, so light and free,
As the sun winked down, "Come join me!"

With every dawn, a zesty jest,
Making friendships that silently blessed.
So here's to mornings, sweet and bright,
In the orchard's embrace, walls take flight.

Juiced Horizons

The sky spills juice, oh what a mess,
My breakfast plate is now in distress.
An orange cat jumps on my lap,
I hope he doesn't think he's a snack!

A toast to mornings, bright and zesty,
My coffee's twitching, oh so testy.
With each sip, I giggle and grin,
As the mug whispers, 'Let's begin!'

The sun's a funny, clumsy clown,
It spills its light all over town.
I trip on shadows, laugh at fate,
In this punchline of a breakfast date.

So here's to dawn, a jester bold,
Turning the ordinary into gold.
Watch the laughs as the world awakes,
In this juicy dance, no one fakes!

A Sunrise in Orange Hues

Awake to hues of orange cheer,
I swear I saw my toast disappear!
The jam has taken quite a jump,
It landed right on my cat's rump!

Pancakes flipping like a circus act,
With syrup rivers, sweet and stacked.
"More napkins!" I shout with glee,
As my breakfast does the cha-cha with me.

The sun's a comedian, bright and free,
With jokes that float through the morning tea.
Each ray a wink, each cloud a grin,
A slapstick show as the day begins.

So bring on the giggles, the fruit parade,
In this kitchen circus that we've made.
With laughter spilling like a morning drink,
Life's a comedy — don't you think?

Fragrant Mornings Unfold

A scent of zest hangs in the air,
My socks were paired — or so I swear!
The blender roars, it's quite a beast,
Or is that just my morning feast?

I trip on toast, the butter flies,
It lands on my dog, who looks surprised.
The fridge is laughing, how very rude,
While fruit conspirators plot their food.

Lemon's giggles bounce off the wall,
As I juggle oranges, I take a fall.
The floor's a slip-and-slide of glee,
As I embrace this morning spree.

Here's to starting days with wit,
In a kitchen where the jokes never quit.
With fragrant mornings bringing delight,
I cheer for breakfast, what a sight!

The Tang of Awakening Light

The light comes creeping, oh so sly,
It tickles my nose and makes me cry.
The toast burns bright, it's doing a dance,
While coffee goes rogue, in its fine romance!

A knife slips and does a little spin,
Hoping to find where the jam has been.
The sun's a trickster, playing games,
With shadows casting silly names.

A grapefruit bursts with laughter loud,
As I attempt to join the crowd.
The table's now a circus ring,
Where breakfast fights, and joy takes wing!

So here's to days that start with fun,
When every breakfast is just begun.
With tangy flavors at play in sight,
In this wild dance of morning light!

Sun-Kissed Citrus Dreams

Awake with lemon zest, a jolly cheer,
Orange socks on toes, I cannot steer.
With grapefruit hats, we dance on air,
Juicy giggles bubble, without a care.

Lemonade rivers flow through my mind,
Citrus giggles and puns, so well-timed.
I tripped on a lime, what a sight to see,
Fell into a vat of sweet tangerine tea.

Bright sunbeams wink, wearing orange shades,
Fruit-fueled laughter in whimsical parades.
Zesty jokes fly, like birds on a spree,
Join the feast of laughter, come sip with me.

As I squeeze my eyes, the sun's a peach,
A zany dance-off with limes, what a reach!
In this world of zests, we roll and spin,
With citrus dreams, let the fun begin!

Aromatic Awakening

The morning air smells of tangy delight,
Pineapple pancakes take flight in my sight.
Wake up the lemons, let laughter unfold,
With citrusy giggles, our stories are told.

The toast sings a tune, it's fragrant and bright,
A syrup of oranges, what pure delight!
I danced with a grapefruit, slipped on its peel,
Oh, morning of fun, what a zestful meal!

Kidding with kiwis, they tickle and tease,
As I squeeze out the juice, it's sure to please.
Juggling these fruits, oh what a bold plan,
What could possibly go wrong? Well, here I am.

So pour out the laughter, let's soak in the sun,
With apples so silly, let's just have some fun.
This fragrant awakening, who wants to sleep?
Join the merry fruit fest, it's ours to keep!

Slices of Dawn's Delight

In the morn, I slice a sweet, juicy dream,
Orange wedges giggle, they burst at the seam.
Peeling back laughter, I pop them with joy,
What mischief awaits with this citrus decoy?

Mimosa rivers flow, can you hear the roar?
Bananas play tag with a charming s'more.
With every bite, I'm swept off my feet,
These slices of dawn, oh, aren't they a treat?

Twirling around with a citrusy grin,
Doughnuts throw sprinkles; let the fun begin!
Citrus confetti flies into the sky,
Happiness drips like syrup, oh my, oh my!

As I sip my juice, the world feels so bright,
Lemons sing lullabies, a wonderful sight.
So come join the feast, with laughter a-plenty,
With slices of dawn, our joy is never empty!

Tangerine Glow on the Horizon

A tangerine glow lights the sky like a flame,
I'm wearing orange pants—this morning's the same.
With a smile made of jelly, I jump out of bed,
Dreaming of fruits and the fun that I'll spread.

I find a banana, all dressed up in style,
It's winked at me twice; let's go for a smile!
Chasing each other down syrupy lanes,
We squeal with delight as each wacky joke reigns.

As suns dance around, my breakfast's a ball,
Sipping on citrus nectar, I'm having a ball.
With oranges juggling up high in the trees,
Life's sweetest moments are caught in the breeze.

So wave at the fruit, let's sing to the dawn,
With laughter, we rise, and the silliness spawns.
In this tangerine glow, where joy never drains,
We revel in fun, and that's all that remains!

Golden Zest Awakening

A lemon squirted on my shoe,
I slipped and danced, oh what a view!
With orange peels upon my head,
I laughed so hard, almost fell dead.

The sun arose, a grapefruit grin,
It winked at me, let the fun begin!
The batches of bright zest on the floor,
Squeezed by my antics, I can't take more!

A lime just rolled and hit a cat,
Who leaped up high, what's wrong with that?
The citrus army makes me cheer,
Their fruity jokes bring smiles here!

So when the morning starts to shine,
I welcome laughter, and some divine.
With silly fruits all round my feet,
My golden zest, oh, what a treat!

Tangerine Dreams at Dawn

A tangerine rolled down the lane,
It stopped to sip the morning rain.
A giggle burst, what splashes fun,
In early light, we run and run.

The sky's a hue of peachy dreams,
I bounced on clouds, or so it seems.
The oranges danced a funny jig,
While I attempted, oh so big!

A fruit parade, oh what a sight,
Bananas juggled in the light.
Pineapples twirled on sunny backs,
While lemons formed some silly hacks.

With laughter ringing out of tune,
The dawn I share with fruity boon.
What joy in bundles, all aglow,
Tangerine dreams, let the fun flow!

Sunlit Citrus Reverie

In the light of dawn's embrace,
A lemon sneezed, began the race.
With juice that squirted, oh what fun,
As zesty smiles had just begun.

A grapefruit leaped, high in the air,
Twisting in loops, with flair and care.
I watched it spin, my eyes went wide,
While laughing loud, I couldn't hide.

The oranges rolled, a cute parade,
In zany hats that I had made.
They strutted by with such a cheer,
These fruity friends, I hold so dear.

With every chuckle, laughter flows,
The sun ignites the funny shows.
In this bright dream where joy takes flight,
Sunlit delights, oh what a sight!

The Morning Citrus Symphony

A sour note from a lime's delight,
Played in a band that feels just right.
With tangerines on trumpets loud,
Making us laugh, oh, what a crowd!

To oranges strumming, caressing light,
Each plucky fruit takes the stage bright.
They played a tune, a silly song,
With zestful beats that rolled along.

Bananas on drums gave one big thump,
And lemons danced with every jump.
Their citrus jokes brought giggles near,
In harmony, their sounds we cheer.

So as the dawn breaks wide and free,
Join in the fun, come laugh with me.
With nature's batch, we sing along,
To breakfast joy, our fruity song!

Glow of the Clementine

In the morning, orange on a plate,
Dancing peels, oh what a fate!
Vitamin C, oh how you shine,
Breakfast of champions, truly divine.

Squeezed by hands, a juicy show,
Splatters flying, oh no, oh no!
Giggles erupt like a fizzy drink,
Who knew fruit could make us think?

Sun-Spill on Juicy Fruit

Lemon drops and lime swings,
Sour faces that laughter brings.
Tangerine laughs with a cheeky grin,
Join the fun, let the joy begin.

Orange juice rivers, flowing free,
Splashing around like a jubilee.
Biting in, oh that zest!
Wake up, world, we're on a quest!

Awakening Citrus Melodies

Peeling back the morning haze,
Singing fruits in a zesty craze.
Melodies dance like a summer breeze,
Tickling noses with fragrant ease.

Lemon-lime lullabies take flight,
Chasing shadows out of sight.
Who knew zest could have a beat?
A fruity jig beneath our feet!

The Essence of a Tangy Dawn

Morning sun with a splash of cheer,
Bouncing citrus, all things clear.
Grapefruit giggles in the soft light,
Spicing up the day, oh what a sight!

Pineapple crowns atop our heads,
Silly hats from fruity spreads.
Juicy jests and citrus fun,
Our fruity frolic has just begun!

Sunlit Citrus Serenade

In the morning light, a lemon winks,
Orange laughs, while grapefruit thinks.
They wear their colors bright and bold,
Jokes of zest in stories told.

Limes roll around, causing a scene,
Silly fruit dancing, looking quite keen.
A peach joins in, twirling with flair,
While tangerines giggle, without a care.

Juicy banter fills the air,
As citrus pals make quite a pair.
A juicy joke, a zesty pun,
This happy crew has just begun.

With every shade, a smile anew,
In this orchard, fun is the view.
So raise a toast to the fruit so bright,
In sunlit glee, they take flight.

Sweet Citrus Euphoria

A tangerine trip, what a delight,
Spinning around, oh what a sight!
Lemonade rivers, sparkling and sweet,
Citrus conundrums, can't be beat!

Mango's mischief lends to the play,
As oranges tumble, rolling away.
With a giggle here and a splash of cheer,
Fruits in frolic bring everyone near.

Each juicy joke lights up the day,
With zestful laughter that just won't stay.
Witty puns fly like juicy glows,
In this land of fruits, anything goes!

So hold your green flags; let the fun start,
In the orchard of laughter, we all take part.
What a funny fiesta, a clementine glee,
In this world of sweetness, we're all meant to be!

Mellow Morning Apricots

As soft sunlight stirs, apricots laugh,
Icy orange slices make a bath.
A giggling peach prances around,
In this mellow morn, joy is found.

Radishes blush, joining the team,
While bananas burst out in a dream.
With a wink from pear, the fun ignites,
Fruits planning tricks from morning to nights.

Lemon drops dance, a silly ballet,
Trombone tunes from a lime bouquet.
Smiles are peeling, as seeds take flight,
In this harvest of humor, all feels just right.

So kick back and chuckle, embrace the play,
In a garden of glee, nothing's in the way.
With every sweet bite, laughter will bloom,
In the mellow morning, joy fills the room.

Radiant Fruitful Dawn

At the dawn, where colors collide,
A melon sings, it can't hide!
Mirthful mangoes take the lead,
In this fruitful moment, giggles proceed.

Bananas in pajamas, looking so fine,
Joining the chorus, a zesty line.
Funny watermelon, always a clown,
In the spotlight, shining, never down.

Grapefruits poke with a sour grin,
While cherries burst forth, ready to spin.
Dancing around in a fruity parade,
In the dawn's embrace, jokes are made.

So savor the laughter, it's juicy and bright,
In the realm of fruit, take flight!
With every chuckle, each fruity speech,
In this radiant dawn, joy's in reach!

Citrus Bliss on the Dawn Breeze

In the morning light, a fruit parade,
Lemons juggling while oranges invade.
Limes on roller skates, what a sight!
Grapefruits in sunglasses, feeling all right.

Tangerines dancing on the grass,
Sipping juice while they take a pass.
Pineapples wearing polka dot ties,
Swinging their tops, oh what a surprise!

The lemon tree starts a stand-up show,
Cracking jokes that only oranges know.
Everyone's laughing, it's quite a scene,
With giggles and laughs, they're all so keen.

As dawn breaks, fruits toast their cheer,
With puns so fresh, we all draw near.
Let's squirt some joy in every bite,
In this fruity world, everything's alright.

Sunrise Over Fruity Fields

In a field of fruit, the morning awakes,
Bananas in shades, sharing some shakes.
Pears doing yoga, striking a pose,
While berries burst forth in colorful clothes.

Grapes are gossiping on the vine,
Trading sweet secrets, oh how they shine!
Kiwis breakdance on the soft, green grass,
While watermelons cheer, "Come join us, alas!"

Citrus confetti floating on breeze,
As the sun peeks over with sparkling tease.
Oranges giggle, calling friends near,
To share in the fun, spreading good cheer.

This fruity fiesta, let laughter flow,
With peels of joy, in the early glow.
Sipping the sunshine, feeling so free,
In this fruity fun, just you and me.

Aromatic Dawn Chorus

Morning melodies from the zesty grove,
With oranges singing, a tune to behold.
Lemons and limes offer their flair,
Creating a chorus that dances in air.

A grapefruit strums on an old guitar,
While cherries chime in from near and far.
Peaches are clapping, keeping the beat,
As rhythm and laughter swirl down the street.

The sun's rays wander, tickling the leaves,
Fruits harmonizing in playful reprieves.
With every note, joy continues to swell,
In this fruity orchestra, all is so well.

Their tunes chase away remnants of night,
Bringing forth fun with every delight.
So raise up a glass of this fragrant cheer,
For in this dawn chorus, happiness is here.

Awakening to Zesty Radiance

A zesty alarm clock made of bright hue,
Grapefruit spins tales, always something new.
Mimosas are giggling as they cheer,
In this morning glow, all worries disappear.

Lemons wear shoes, shuffle to a beat,
While splashes of orange dance on their feet.
Bouncing bananas join the parade,
In this juicy jubilee, nothing's delayed.

The sun beams down, bringing laughter in rays,
As peaches propose silly morning plays.
The zesty fun never seems to dim,
In this playful dawn, we'll all join in.

So grab a slice and toast to this day,
Where fruits bring joy in their own quirky way.
With colors and giggles, the world feels bright,
Awakening to laughter, everything's right.

Morning Mist and Citrus Burst

In the morning mist, I slipped on a peel,
Orange juice fountain, a slippery deal.
Squeezed all my laughter, out flooded the floor,
What a zesty wake-up, who could ask for more?

Chasing the cat, in a tangy ballet,
He dodged the lime slice, oh, what a display!
With a twist of a lemon, I danced with delight,
Morning treats juggling, what a fruity flight!

Pineapple joins in, a wobbly friend,
Together we giggle, no need to pretend.
A fruit salad chorus, we laugh and we sing,
A zany fiesta, oh, the joy that we bring!

So raise up your glasses, toast to the day,
Every drop of sunshine, let it play and sway.
With fruity mishaps, let's cheer and let's burst,
We'll snack on the humor, quench our thirst!

A Wakeful Citrus Chord

Alarm clock's a lemon, it zings and it zaps,
As I reach for my juice, life overlaps.
Mornings are tango, a citrusy spin,
Stumbling on snacks, oh let the fun begin!

A grapefruit serenade, zesty and bright,
In this juicy chaos, nothing feels right.
Balancing oranges, a juggler's delight,
Seeing stars in my cereal, oh, what a sight!

Squeezed out the sleep, laughter's on blast,
In shade of an orange, my worries are cast.
I tiptoe through tangles, a breakfast parade,
With squirts of absurdity, joy's getting made!

So, belt it out loud, let the melody ring,
In the echo of fruit, our hearts take to wing.
With a spoonful of humor, we savor our thrill,
Every morning adventure, a juice-filled spill!

The Aroma of Citrus Dawn

The sun peeks through zest, a wake-up surprise,
With lemons on limb, I catch the good skies.
Freshly squeezed dreams, a toast with a grin,
In a world full of laughter, let the zany begin!

Grapefruit's my partner, we tango and twirl,
Dancing on toast, watch those flavors unfurl.
Syrupy giggles, we skip down the lane,
With each fruity step, we banish the mundane!

The aroma's a hug, bright and quite bold,
It wraps 'round my laughter, a patchwork of gold.
I high-five a lemon, it slaps back with glee,
Citrus sunrise shadows, come join the spree!

So raise up your forks, let's feast on the fun,
Each bite is a chuckle; our day's just begun.
With laughter and flavors, we cheerfully roam,
In this sweet, tangy land, we make a fine home!

Warm Citrus Tides

On a wave of warm zest, the day starts to gleam,
Surfing the flavors, it's all like a dream.
Citrus spills out like a splash in the sun,
Waves of bright laughter; hey, this is fun!

Grab a grapefruit surfboard, ride on that zest,
Wipeout on oranges, oh, what a jest!
Limes in the skies are the clouds that we chase,
Citrusy giggles, we laugh through the race!

In a punchy tide pool, our worries dissolve,
With every sip taken, our spirits evolve.
We krump and we splash in this fruity delight,
With sunbeam smiles, everything feels just right!

So, pack up your laughter, let's charge through the day,
With warmth of the citrus to light up our way.
We ride on the waves of sun-drizzled cheer,
In our tangy adventure, together, we steer!

Freshly Squeezed Mornings

Waking up with a zesty grin,
The sun's a slice of orange skin!
Pajamas sticking, I trip on my shoes,
Stumbling over dreams and morning news.

Juice drips down, a sticky delight,
My hair's reminiscent of a fruit fight.
Spilled coffee dances, a swirling mess,
Yet somehow, it feels like a citrus fest!

The toast pops up, flying through air,
Butter lands with a bold, dramatic flair.
I sip my drink, a laugh on repeat,
As breakfast juggles, a fruity feat!

Oh, freshly squeezed, come play along,
Morning's a clown, a zestful song.
The day begins with a juicy twist,
Where every sip is a fruity tryst.

Citrus Bliss Colliding with Dawn

The rooster crows with a grapefruit smile,
Inhale that sun, can you feel its style?
My slippers squeak like a lemon sprite,
As I chase my thoughts, they take flight!

A blender whirls in a fruity spree,
I'm diving deep in a smoothie sea.
Bananas giggle, berries entwine,
What a morning, sweet and divine!

Lemonade dreams dance through my head,
While toast pops up, like a warm bed.
I trip over jellies, my grin on display,
Who knew mornings could taste like play?

Colliding flavors make the day bright,
Citrus sparks in a laugh-filled light.
I toast to the sunrise, fresh and bold,
Every sip tells a story yet to be told.

Awakening in Orchard Colors

Awake with the laugh of a tangy hue,
Bouncing from dreams that were sweet like stew.
My socks mismatched, a color parade,
In this orchard of chaos, I'm unafraid!

The apples and oranges plan a spree,
While lemons plot tricks just for me.
I stumble on toast that dares to leap,
In this morning orchard, I can't help but peep!

Juicy giggles fill the ripe air,
As I juggle my breakfast without a care.
The sun peeks in with a playful wink,
I trip on laughter more than a drink!

Orchestra of flavors, performing with glee,
The day unfurls so spectacularly.
I stumble, I laugh, perhaps even fall,
In this orchard of colors, I'm having a ball!

Radiance of the Lemon Grove

Beneath the sun where the lemons thrive,
I wake each day, feeling so alive.
With mishaps galore, my hair's in a twist,
What a citrus start — you get the gist!

The toast is dancey, it jumps on the plate,
An orange squeezes in, just to celebrate.
My chair's a trampoline, I bounce with cheer,
As sunlight spills in, it's almost sincere!

A tangle of zest, a riddle of rays,
This morning chaos sets the pace for my days.
I sip and I chuckle, humor in play,
In this lemon grove, it's a fruity ballet!

Oh, what a scene as limes roll away,
Mornings are sweeter in this joyful array.
I'll tease and delight, with each sip I take,
In the glow of the grove, let's dance 'til we break!

www.ingramcontent.com/pod-product-compliance
Lightning Source LLC
Chambersburg PA
CBHW070309120526
44590CB00017B/2595